THE BOOK BAG TREASURY OF
LITERARY
QUIZZES

THE BOOK BAG TREASURY OF
LITERARY QUIZZES

THE EDITORS OF The Washington Post
Book World

INTRODUCTION BY
BRIGITTE WEEKS

CHARLES SCRIBNER'S SONS

New York

Library of Congress Cataloging in Publication Data

Main entry under title:

The book bag treasury of literary quizzes.

1. Literary recreations. I. Washington post.
GV1493.B62   1984   793.73   84-3901
ISBN 0-684-18129-0

1 3 5 7 9 11 13 15 17 19   F/P   20 18 16 14 12 10 8 6 4 2

Printed in the United States of America.

Book Bag logo by Michael David Brown
© Washington Post Book World

Contents

Introduction

When *The Washington Post Book World* became a tabloid magazine in August 1979, we wanted to learn more about those loyal, literate readers that we assumed we were serving week by week. We only got letters when we made them mad, but we knew they were out there. So was born the Book Bag competition.

We intended to ask a bookish, tricky question whose answer would range in difficulty from the obvious to the obscure. We also hoped to make the contest quirky, wide-ranging, and fun. At this writing we are publishing Book Bag Number 221. Along the way, Book Bag has gathered fanatical readers who never miss a Sunday, satisfied winners who highly prize their scarlet book bags emblazoned with the *Book World* logo, and some disgruntled souls who have argued with our answers and uncovered hitherto unknown variants of little known stories.

On one memorable occasion we ran a question on the military ranks of various literary heroes. We answered our own question slightly inaccurately and military Washington rose up in wrath to point out the difference between—was it a commander and a captain? Or an ensign and a seaman? We licked our wounds and took K.P. (The question—with, we hope, the correct answer—appears in this book.)

Here then is the best of Book Bag, a treasury of questions ranked by how difficult we judged them. They range from "one book" (relatively easy, these shouldn't drive you to the nearest library); "two book" (demanding a little mental gnashing of teeth); and "three book" (these stumped at least half of *Book World*'s editors).

In the history of the competition only two questions have received NO correct answers. They have been allotted "four books" and they appear as a kind of grand finale. We'd love to offer book bags as prizes to those *Book Bag Treasury* readers who solve the four bookers, but at one *Book World* meeting an editor related an anecdote that made us realize that that way madness lay: In 1905, Edgar Wallace wrote a novel called *The Four Just Men*. It contained no solution to how the Just Men had murdered the British foreign secretary and Wallace offered, at

2

his own expense, a prize of £500 for the correct solution. Unfortunately, so many enterprising readers came up with the answer that Wallace lost quite a large sum of money. So—satisfaction is your only reward if you solve the two four-book questions.

Half of *The Book Bag Treasury* is made up of questions that have already been published in *The Washington Post Book World,* while the others have been generated especially for this book by an enthusiastic editorial staff.

The group of literary trivia enthusiasts who have twisted their minds to create this book includes Reid Beddow, Alice Digilio, Michael Dirda and myself. Anton Mueller has contributed invaluable research. Although we have tried for accuracy at every level, we know enough to recognize that errors stalk the wariest editor. We take credit for the accuracy and so must accept blame for any blunders.

—Brigitte Weeks

～ Writing ～
Around the World

📖———————————————————————

The sister of two eminent men of letters, this diarist was unhealthy most of her short life and railed against her fate and woman's lot, describing herself as "an appendage to five cushions and three shawls" and writing, "It is an immense loss to have all robust and sustaining expletives refined away from one!" Who was she?

📖———————————————————————

Latin American literature has dazzled the world in the last two decades. Often it confronts the cultural interaction between the Americas, North and South. Who wrote about a little Argentinian boy Toto and his fantasies about a silver screen goddess? Can you can name her as well?

Alice James, the sister of Henry and William

Manuel Puig wrote about the film goddess in Betrayed by Rita Hayworth.

■

In Victorian London a famous man of letters
lent the manuscript of his new book to a political philosopher to read. The latter's housemaid
mistakenly tossed the manuscript into the fire;
thus perished years of work. The man of letters
had to rewrite the whole thing. Who were the
man of letters and the philosopher and what was
the manuscript?

■■

Originally a lyric poet, this British author later
turned to fiction. Among her works are *The
Unlit Lamp* and *The Well of Loneliness*. Because of its sympathetic treatment of lesbians,
the latter book was banned in England. Who
was this writer?

■■

The answer to his past lies hidden in this song:

Sugarman don't leave me here.
Cotton balls to choke me
O Sugarman don't leave me here
Buckra's arms to yoke me. . .

His name is Milkman, his aunt is Pilate and his
father is Dead. Who is this character, and in
what novel did he appear?

Thomas Carlyle lent his manuscript of The French Revolution *to John Stuart Mill, whose maid burned it. Carlyle rewrote the book.*

Radclyffe Hall was the author of The Well of Loneliness, *which caused a sensation when it was published in 1928.*

Macon "Milkman" Dead, from Toni Morrison's Song of Solomon

Describing his own work, this African author wrote, "As long as one people sit on another and are deaf to their cry, so long will understanding and peace elude all of us." His acclaimed first novel, *Things Fall Apart,* relates the tragic encounter of traditional Ibo life in Nigeria with Christianity and colonialism. Who is he?

Three women booksellers—an American and a Frenchwoman in France and another American in the United States—were important to the international fame and success of James Joyce in the 1920s and '30s. Who were they?

A famous American author was born when Halley's comet appeared in 1835 and died, as he had predicted, when it appeared again in 1910. "It will be the greatest disappointment of my life if I don't go out with Halley's Comet," he had written. "The Almighty has said, no doubt: 'Now here are two unaccountable freaks; they came in together, they must go out together.' " Who was he?

Chinua Achebe, one of several Nigerian novel-
ists of note—another is Wole Soyinka. Their
country is the most populous in Africa.

Sylvia Beach was the proprietor of the book-
store Shakespeare and Company, which pub-
lished Ulysses*; Adrienne Monnier, who ran La*
Maison des Amis des Livres across the street,
helped promote Joyce among French writers
and intellectuals; and Frances Steloff owned
the Gotham Book Mart in New York City, a
center for James Joyce enthusiasts in America.

Mark Twain. Incidentally, King Edward VII
died around the same time as Twain and The
Times *of London, à propos of the comet, was*
able to quote Julius Caesar*: "When beggars die,*
there are no comets seen; The heavens them-
selves blaze forth the death of princes."

~ Who's Who? ~

🔖🔖🔖————————————————————————

The only child of a great banker and of a woman beloved by Edward Gibbon, she possessed a passionate heart and a brilliant mind. Around her collected the most sparkling wits of France, Germany and England. Before the French Revolution her salon was a hotbed of political discussion. Napoleon allowed her to return to Paris from exile after the Revolution, though he later demanded that she keep 40 leagues from the capital. Benjamin Constant's *Adolphe* chronicles in part his destructive passion for this demanding mistress. Her writing was as celebrated as her conversation, and her most famous book introduced German culture to the French and helped define the concept of "Romanticism." Who was this woman and what was the title of this book in its original language?

Madame de Stael, author of De l'Allemagne

In general, men are not noted for their extravagance of dress. However, there are a few fellows in fiction who can be immediately recognized by their distinctive garb. Who wears the following?

a. The skin of a lion he has slain.
b. Yellow stockings and cross-garters.
c. A deerstalker hat.

"A little learning is a dangerous thing;/Drink deep, or taste not the Pierian spring," was penned by a famous poet of Augustan England. A fellow Englishman who was a 20th-century novelist borrowed part of this verse for the title of his autobiography, *A Little Learning*. Name both authors.

This unhappy lawyer worked in a government office in Prague processing workmen's compensation claims. His three uncompleted novels, *Der Prozess, Das Schloss* and *Amerika,* form a brilliant trilogy of human isolation and pathos. Who was he?

a. *Hercules*
b. *Malvolio*
c. *Sherlock Holmes*

Alexander Pope and Evelyn Waugh. The Pierian spring refers to the reputed home of the Muses in classical antiquity.

Franz Kafka

Hunger, a chilling study of the disintegration of a human mind under the stress of physical deprivation, was written by Norway's most famous modern novelist. A vagabond for much of his life, he lived briefly in Minnesota at the turn of the century. Later he was condemned for welcoming the Nazi invaders of Norway in 1940. What was his name?

This famous writer was married three times, appeared on stage semi-topless, had a lesbian love affair, opened a beauty shop, and wrote a novel that made Proust weep. Who was she?

What writer studied law in her father's office but could not take the bar examination, insisted on omitting the word "obey" from her marriage vows, helped organize the first women's rights convention in 1848 and with publisher Susan B. Anthony edited a militant feminist magazine?

Knut Hamsun. In April 1940, when the Germans invaded Norway, he sullied his reputation among his compatriots by supporting the puppet government of Vikdun Quisling.

The French writer Colette. The novel was Mitsou.

Elizabeth Cady Stanton was this suffragist writer. She died in 1902, two decades before women got the vote in the United States.

~ Name Calling ~

The title of this 19th-century Utopian satire is the imaginary land where it takes place. Yet when its name is spelled backward, it takes place nowhere. Who is the author of this novel and what is its title?

In which novels do these three lonely "last" heroes appear, and who created them?

Uncas, in *The Last* .... by ....
Oliver Alden in *The Last* .... by ....
Monroe Stahr, in *The Last* .... by ....

If you were having "An Agony in Eight Fits," what would you be doing?

Samuel Butler was the author of Erewhon.

———————————————

The Last of the Mohicans, *by James Fenimore Cooper*
The Last Puritan, *by George Santayana*
The Last Tycoon, *by F. Scott Fitzgerald*

———————————————

You would be reading Lewis Carroll's The Hunting of the Snark. *"An Agony in Eight Fits" is its subtitle.*

In English, the title is literally translated as *The Tailer Re-Patches*. This famous 19th-century book chronicles the life and opinions of one Diogenes Teufelsdrockh of Weissnichtwo, who asserts that reality is embodied solely within infinite and mystical perspectives. By what title do we now know this treatise?

"Daisy, Daisy, give me your answer do." And here's a Daisy-chain of heroines who might give the following replies. Name the novels they grace:

a. You can see my house if you look across the harbor.
b. I represent one segment of bohemian literary Manhattan in the '20s.
c. I'm a flirt from Schenectady.

Authors often (wisely) change the original titles of their books; for instance, Sinclair Lewis first planned to call *Main Street* "The Village Virus." Tolstoy named one of his books "All's Well that Ends Well." By what title do we know this novel today?

Sartor Resartus, *by Thomas Carlyle*

a. The Great Gatsby, *by F. Scott Fitzgerald*
b. I Thought of Daisy, *by Edmund Wilson*
c. Daisy Miller, *by Henry James*

War and Peace

◧◧◧————————————————

The title of this novel refers to the procedures of an auction, in particular the selling of an esoteric collection of stamps left to one Oedipa Maas by her former lover. As Maas investigates these stamps, she stumbles upon an enigmatic underground postal network called WASTE, part of the world-wide conspiracy known as the Tristero System. Who created this philatelic intrigue and what is the novel called?

◧◧————————————————

What 20th-century satire is subtitled "The Illuminating Diary of a Professional Lady"?

◧◧◧————————————————

Most everyone has heard of Margaret Sidey's *The Five Little Peppers* and Agatha Christie's *Ten Little Indians*. Here are some other quantitative book titles. Fill in their authors and the missing figures.

......*Pillars of Wisdom*, by ....
The ...... Steps, by ....
The Moon and ...... pence, by ....
.... *Coaches Waiting*, by ....
The ...... Clocks, by ....

Thomas Pynchon wrote The Crying of Lot 49.

Anita Loos' Gentlemen Prefer Blondes

Seven Pillars of Wisdom, *by T. E. Lawrence*
The 39 Steps, *by John Buchan*
The Moon and Sixpence, *by W. Somerset Maugham*
Nine Coaches Waiting, *by Mary Stewart*
The 13 Clocks, *by James Thurber*

◧◧◧──────────────────

What English novelist, whose fantasies have
gained a cult following his death, also illustrated
an edition of Lewis Carroll's *Alice in Wonderland*? What were the two most popular books he
himself wrote?

◧◧──────────────────

Helen, thy beauty is to me
Like those Nicean banks of yore,
That gently, o'er a perfumed sea,
The weary, way-worn wanderer bore
To his own native shore.

These lines, from the poem "To Helen," by
Edgar Allan Poe, were pirated by the protago-
nist of a Hollywood novel who offered them as
original verse in order to impress his girlfriend.
What is the title of the novel?

◧◧◧──────────────────

What 20th-century autobiographical work bor-
rows themes and characters from John Bunyan's
17th-century masterpiece, *The Pilgrim's Progress*?

Mervyn Peake illustrated Alice in Wonderland. *His own two most popular titles were* Titus Groan *and* Gormenghast.

The Loved One, *by Evelyn Waugh*

The Enormous Room, *by e.e. cummings*

◨◨◨————————————————————

Complete this floral bouquet of titles.

.... *Clay*
The ..... Tattoo
The Blue ......
.......Wine
.......and Goldmund

◨◨◨————————————————————

Macbeth's famous soliloquy beginning, "She should have died hereafter" (V,v) has inspired many and furnished others with titles for their books. Name the titles the following authors have borrowed from the Bard on this account.

a. Aldous Huxley
b. H.M.Tomlinson
c. Rose Macaulay
d. William Faulkner

Violet Clay, *by Gail Godwin*
The Rose Tattoo, *by Tennessee Williams*
The Blue Dahlia, *by Raymond Chandler*
Dandelion Wine, *by Ray Bradbury*
Narcissus and Goldmund, *by Herman Hesse*

---

a. Brief Candles
b. All Our Yesterdays
c. Told by an Idiot
d. The Sound and the Fury

Reading the Heart

Romantic poet Samuel Taylor Coleridge was, for many years, involved in an unhappy marriage, the problems of which were compounded by his impossible love for Sarah Hutchinson, the sister-in-law of William Wordsworth, his friend and literary contemporary. In 1802, his torment inspired Coleridge to write a poem. What is its title?

Before World War I a beautiful boy had become so enraptured by her body and all which it received or touched that he had begged to wear her pearls. She was one of the most sensually knowing courtesans to appear in 20th-century literature. Who was she and from whose imagination did she spring?

*"Dejection: An Ode," which opens with an epi-
graph taken from "The Ballad of Sir Patrick
Spens":*

*Late, late yestreen I saw the new Moon,
With the old Moon in her arms;
And I fear, I fear, my master dear!
We shall have a deadly storm.*

---

*Colette created Léa, intimate to the boy Chéri.
There were two Chéri novels:* Chéri *and* The
Last of Chéri.

■■■

Beginning with an investigation of the Tristan
legend, this French author traces the legacy of
Western love to contemporary times. Along the
way he arrives at many conclusions, none more
important than the following: "Happy love has
no history. Romance only comes into existence
where love is fatal, frowned upon, doomed by
life itself. What stirs the lyrical poets to their
finest flights is neither the delight of the senses
nor the fruitful contentment of the settled couple; not the satisfaction of love, but its passion.
And passion means suffering. There we have the
fundamental fact." Who expressed this thought
and in what work?

■■■

"It is the Man and the Woman united that make
the compleat human Being. . . . But . . . in all
your amours you should prefer old women to
young ones." These lines are part of an 18th-
century essay proclaiming the virtues of older
mistresses. Judged too indecent to print at the
time, it was unknown to the public until this
century. Who was its author?

Denis de Rougemont, Love in the Western World

Benjamin Franklin. Ben had quite a time with the aristocratic ladies at the court of Louis XVI while his wife, Deborah Read, stayed home in Philadelphia.

Hester Prynne, in Nathaniel Hawthorne's *The Scarlet Letter,* is only one in a long line of literary adulterers. A 1930s British mystery romance, a 19th-century Russian novel, and a 19th-century French novel all have eponymous characters who commit adultery. Name them and their authors.

Born in Verona, this poet died very young, 33 at the oldest. He loved a woman named Clodia, wife of Q. Metellus Celer, whom he celebrated under the name, Lesbia. In his poems, one can trace the path his heart took in the course of their affair, from intoxication and tenderness, to anguish, and ultimately, to loathing and contempt. After their final parting, he traveled to his brother's grave and wrote the lament, "Ave atque vale." Who was he?

Who flirted with the Tarleton twins, married three times and wound up alone?

Rebecca *by Daphne du Maurier*, Anna Kare-nina *by Leo Tolstoy, and* Madame Bovary *by Gustave Flaubert. The ladies ended violently. Rebecca died in a fire, Anna threw herself under a train, and Madame Bovary poisoned herself.*

Catullus, whose love poetry has still the power to move. Some lines from "Carmina":

Let us live and love, my Lesbia, and value at a penny all the talk of old men. Suns may set and rise again: for us, when our brief light has set, there's the sleep of one everlasting night. Give me a thousand kisses.

Scarlett O'Hara. But, alone, she took an opti-mistic note, "After all, tomorrow is another day" and "There never was a man I couldn't get."

The tradition of love at first sight (called a *coup de foudre,* or "thunderclap" in a wonderful French idiom) has few greater proponents than the poets who composed the following lines, which are here given in translation:

And still I bless the day, the hour, the place,
When first so high mine eyes I dared to rear;
And say, "fond heart, thy gratitude declare,
That then thou had'st the privilege to gaze.
'Twas she inspired the tender thought of love
Which points to heaven . . ."

She was dressed in a very noble colour, a decorous and delicate crimson, tied with a girdle and trimmed in a manner suited to her tender age. The moment I saw her I say in all truth that the vital spirit, which dwells in the inmost depth of the heart, began to tremble so violently that I felt the vibration alarmingly in all my pulse. . .

Who are the two poets, and the women they praise?

Of the two examples of love at first sight, the first begining "And still I bless the day . . ." was written by Petrarch in honor of Laura; and the second beginning "She was dressed in a very noble colour" was written by Dante in praise of Beatrice.

Love, as Robert Burns thought and as we have come to believe, is "like a red, red rose"; but who would think to compare two lovers to a pair of "stiff twin compasses"?

"If all the world and love were young" begins a beautiful pastoral love song. The song, a poem, was written as a lover's reply to her suitor's passionate address contained in another poem which concludes, "If these delights thy mind may move/Then live with me and be my love." Name the two poems, the address and the reply, and the poets who penned them.

Rejecting the veil, this Hispano-Arabic poet was the ruling Cordovan khalif's daughter. Mistress of a literary salon, she took as her lover the finest writer of classical Arabic poetry in Andalusia. Much of their liaison was carried out in verse. Who were they?

In "A Valediction: Forbidding Mourning" John Donne writes of the souls of two lovers:

If they be two, they are two so
As stiff twin compasses are two;
Thy soul, the fixt foot, makes no show
To move, but doth, if th' other do.

Sir Walter Raleigh wrote "The Nymph's Reply to the Shepherd" in response to Christopher Marlowe's "The Passionate Shepherd to His Love."

Wallada and Ibn Zaidun

▌▌_____

Most of us prefer happy endings. However, some
authors take their cue from *Romeo and Juliet*
and give us unconsummated romances instead.
In what novels do the following couples go their
separate ways?

a. Ellen Olenska and Newland Archer
b. Lady Brett Ashley and Jake Barnes
c. Maggie Tulliver and Stephen Guest

▌▌_____

In what dictionary can we find the following
definitions: Alone—in bad company; Love—a
temporary insanity curable by marriage; Marriage—a master, a mistress and two slaves, making in all, two.

a. Edith Wharton's The Age of Innocence
b. Ernest Hemingway's The Sun Also Rises
c. George Eliot's The Mill on the Floss

Ambrose Bierce's The Devil's Dictionary. *He
also provided the following definition of Cynic:
"a blackguard whose faulty vision sees things as
they are, not as they ought to be."*

~ Under ~
an English Heaven

▐▐▐————————————————————————

I am a police-court judge who wrote about two Toms. Who am I? And who were they?

▐————————————————————————

Cynicism about the ineffectualness and callousness of government bureaucracies is not a new phenomenon, by any means. In what 19th-century British novel, by whom, does "The Circumlocution Office" play a part?

▐▐————————————————————————

In *Jane Eyre,* Charlotte Bronte told the story of the second Mrs. Rochester. Bertha, the first Mrs. Rochester, had to wait until 1966 for her tale to be told. Who told it in what novel?

Henry Fielding wrote Tom Jones *and the play* Tom Thumb the Great.

"The Circumlocution Office" that Charles Dickens wrote about in Little Dorrit *operated under the credo "How not to do it."*

In Wide Sargasso Sea *Jean Rhys imaginatively reconstructs the girlhood and marriage of Antoinette Bertha Cosway, the mysterious first Mrs. Rochester of* Jane Eyre.

◨◨◨——————————————

Terrorism is a familiar theme in Western literature. In which two English novels, one published in 1907, the other in 1908, does terrorism figure prominently?

◨◨————————————————

Left alone to make her way in life, she practiced self-reliance before it was fashionable for women. She moved to a European town and earned her bread and shelter teaching school. For a short season, the fates seemed to relent. A true lover emerged and love blossomed. Then, in one of the most powerful surprise endings of English fiction, all ease and future promise are dashed aside. Who was the character who spoke through a veil of loss, and who is the author who turned in this her last novel to confront that which forever remained unrealized?

In Joseph Conrad's The Secret Agent *(1907), Mr. Verloc, an "agent provocateur," is assigned to spy on anarchists in London. Posing as a shopkeeper, he makes plans to bomb the Greenwich Observatory, a deed sufficiently irrational and shocking to stir up public opinion against the anarchists. His plans run amok when the man he enlists to carry the bomb, his wife's brother, stumbles and blows himself to smithereens. Verloc's wife avenges her much loved and innocent brother by killing her husband.*

The Man Who Was Thursday *by G.K. Chesterton (1908) tells the story of a terrorist group and its ruling Central Anarchist Council. Lucian Gregory, anarchist and poet, aspires to be elected to the group but is ultimately disappointed. The irony the book exploits is that Lucian is the only true anarchist; all the others are informants.*

Lucy Snowe in Charlotte Bronte's Villette

Shakespeare had two Portias—the beautiful, brilliant heiress of Belmont in *The Merchant of Venice,* and the tragic, noble wife of Brutus in *Julius Caesar.* More than 300 years later, the Anglo-Irish novelist Elizabeth Bowen created another Portia. In which novel did she appear?

For many years the literary editor of *The Listener,* this author was extremely close to E.M. Forster. Of his four books Christopher Isherwood wrote, "Each in its different way is a masterpiece." Two of these works are based on the life of his beautiful Alsatian, Queenie; another records his impressions of India; and the last is a family memoir that reveals his father led a secret life, complete with a second set of children. Who was he and what were the titles of the four books described here?

Portia appears in The Death of the Heart *as the illegitimate 16-year-old girl who comes to live with her half brother after the death of her mother. Her characteristic innocence and idealism are tempered when she falls in love with the callow, insensitive Eddie, a young man who plays whimsically with her passions and has eyes for another.*

J.R. Ackerley edited The Listener *and was the author of* My Dog Tulip, We Think the World of You, Hindoo Holiday *and* My Father and Myself.

This modern novel depicts a vision of the future in which violence and alienation have led to the emergence of a new language, including such curious words as "bezoommy," "viddy" and "sharp." Name, if you can, my "droogs," the title of the novel and define the meaning of the four neologisms above.

This physically deformed man of letters was one of the first Englishmen to demonstrate that literature could be a gainful profession. An intimate of Swift, Gay and Viscount Bolingbroke, he penned a brilliant mock-epic on the theft of a curl. Who was this "wicked wasp of Twickenham"?

In A Clockwork Orange, *Anthony Burgess looks into a future where language has changed and "bezoommy" means mad, "viddy" means to see or look, "sharp" means female and "droog" friend.*

Though a severe illness in childhood stunted his growth (he grew to be a mere four feet six inches) and left him crook-backed and tubercular, Alexander Pope was the literary dictator of his age. Poet, critic, philosopher, he was wont to attack his contemporaries, often spitefully, as, for example, his attack on Joseph Addison in "Epistle to Dr. Arbuthnot." This earned him the name the Wicked Wasp of Twickenham, from the village in which he lived.

An exile for much of his life, this Englishman called his existence "a savage enough pilgrimage." In his novels, poetry and short stories, he examined human relationships and, above all, the proper basis of marriage. Four women deeply influenced him: his mother, Jessie Chambers, Louie Burrows, and the cousin of Baron von Richthofen, whom he married. Who was he?

Recently rediscovered, this author created such memorable characters as the self-centered Leonora Eyre, the elegant Wilmet Forsyth, the delightful Mildred Lathbury and the intellectual Emma Howick. Before retiring to an Oxfordshire cottage, the writer also worked as an editor at the International African Institute. Who was she, and which books feature these literary ladies?

Despite common misperceptions, D.H. Lawrence was less of a womanizer than womanized. The four most influential women in his life were: His mother, on whom the protective Gertrude Morel of Sons and Lovers *was based; Jessie Chambers, who was the model for Miriam Leivers of* Sons and Lovers *and the author of* D.H. Lawrence: A Personal Record; *Louisa (Louie) Burrows, who was one of the prototypes of Ursula in* The Rainbow, *and the subject of some of Lawrence's most intense love poems; and Frieda von Richthofen, whom he married after her divorce from Professor Ernest Weekley, his former French tutor. Lawrence described their stormy but happy marriage in his writings, especially in the collection of poems,* Look! We Have Come Through.

Barbara Pym created Leonora Eyre in The Sweet Dove Died; *Wilmet Forsyth in* A Glass of Blessings; *Mildred Lathbury in* Excellent Women; *and Emma Howick in* A Few Green Leaves.

∽ Tidings of ∽ Comfort and Joy

William Sidney Porter wrote a short story, which has enjoyed enduring popularity, that represented the spirit of Christmas giving. What is the story, and what is Porter's better-known name?

The feast of Hanukkah commemorates the victory over the Syrians by a mighty Jewish warrior who then purified the Temple. Later he was slain at the battle of Elasa. His story is told in several books of the Apocrypha. Who was this character, and who wrote about him (in Greek) in the Apocrypha?

William Sidney Porter (1862-1910) wrote his popular Christmas short story "The Gift of the Magi" (1906) under the pseudonym of O. Henry.

Judas Maccabaeus' exploits were commemorated by Jason of Cyrene.

A famous scholar of Oriental and Greek literature is remembered today not for his linguistic studies but for a delightful poem he penned:

He was dressed all in fur from his head to his
    foot,
And his clothes were all tarnished with ashes
    and soot;
A bundle of toys he had flung on his back,
And he looked like a pedlar just opening his
    pack.

Who wrote these lines and what was his immortal poem?

"Christmas won't be Christmas without any presents." Their Papa serving as a chaplain to the Union forces, four sisters believe they have a bleak holiday ahead. In what famous story do these young ladies appear and what are their names?

Clement Clarke Moore (1779-1863) described St. Nicholas in "A Visit from St. Nicholas" (often misnamed "The Night Before Christmas"), which was first published in the Troy, N.Y., Sentinel. *Moore taught at the General Theological Seminary in New York from 1823 to 1850.*

The March sisters: Meg, Jo, Beth, and Amy from Little Women, *by Louisa May Alcott*

◗◗◗———————————————————

In keeping with parsimonious times, this compiler of quotations stated, à la Calvin Coolidge, "Christmas is over and Business is Business." Who is this Scrooge-like individual?

◗◗◗———————————————————

Usually known for his *A Christmas Carol* and that thoroughly transformed Ebenezer Scrooge, Charles Dickens wrote about the holiday in other books as well. Where does this passage come from?

"My best of wishes for your merry Christmases and your happy New Years, your long lives and your true prosperities. Worth twenty pound good if they are delivered as I send them. Remember? Here's a final prescription added, 'To be taken for life.' "

◗———————————————————

"One Christmas was so much like another, in those years around the seatown corner now and out of all sound except the distant speaking of the voices I sometimes hear a moment before sleep . . . ." These lovely lines begin what famous piece about youth and memory?

Franklin Pierce Adams, an American columnist known simply as F.P.A. His column, called "The Conning Tower," appeared in several New York papers from 1913 to 1941.

———————

"Dr. Marigold's Prescriptions" appeared in 1865 as the extra Christmas number for All the Year Round, *the weekly periodical which Dickens began in 1859 and carried on until his death in 1870.*

———————

Dylan Thomas wrote A Child's Christmas in Wales, *a lyrical memoir about the excited goings-on at Christmas time in a small Welsh town by the sea very much like his own native Swansea.*

Then he slithered and slunk, with a smile most
    unpleasant,
Around the whole room, and he took every
present!
Popguns! And bicycles! Roller skates! Drums!
Checkerboards! Tricycles! Popcorn! and plums!
And he stuffed them in bags. Then the . . . . .
    very nimbly,
Stuffed all the bags, one by one, up the
chimbley!

Who is the culprit that wrecked Santa's plan,
and who invented the nasty fiend?

📖📖📖————————————————

I did not know she'd take it so,
Or else I'd never dared:
Although the bliss was worth the blow,
I did not know she'd take it so,
She stood beneath the mistletoe
So long I thought she cared;
I did not know she'd take it so,
Or else I'd never dared.

What early 20th-century black poet wrote this
verse?

It was the Grinch, created by Dr. Seuss in How The Grinch Stole Christmas, *who wrecked Santa's plan and stole all the Christmas presents.*

Countee Cullen wrote those lines in "Under the Mistletoe." In Cullen's verse, black poetry found one of its gentler voices of the first half of the 20th century; untouched by the bitterness of many later black poets, he wrote:

Call me a traitor if you must. . .
I'll hear your censure as your praise,
For never shall the clan
Confine my singing to its ways
Beyond the ways of man.

∿ Bookies ∿

◖◗◖

In the annals of 20th-century literary awards, what is significant about the years 1914, 1918 and 1935?

◖

Which of the Founding Fathers, partly out of a need for money, arranged a lucrative sale of his books to the new Library of Congress?

◖◗

What do Margaret Mitchell's *Gone With the Wind*, Emily Bronte's *Wuthering Heights*, M. I. Lermontov's *A Hero of Our Time*, and Lady Murasaki's *The Tale of Genji* have in common?

In these years no Nobel Prize in literature was awarded.

Thomas Jefferson

These are the only novels their authors completed.

Goethe's *Faust*, Thomas Mann's *The Magic Mountain*, Joyce's *Ulysses* and Nathaniel Hawthorne's "Young Goodman Brown" all include scenes that take place on or are inspired by a certain evil night of the year, a night when witches held festival. Name this night that is not Halloween, and the calendar day it falls on.

The Waste Land, T.S. Eliot's long, influential poem on the desiccation of Western civilization, was published in 1922. The original draft of the poem was bought by a New York collector of art and literature, who befriended and financially supported Eliot and many other modernist writers, including Pound and Joyce. Who was he?

This 11th-century Oriental court figure wrote what is often regarded as the world's first novel. Who was she, and what is the title of her work?

*Walpurgis Night (*Walpurgisnacht*) or the Witches' Sabbath takes place on the eve of May Day. In Hawthorne's allegorical version, Goodman Brown leaves his wife Faith to venture into the forest and a meeting with the Devil and his congregation of the fallen. The scene for these dark festivities is seen vividly: "At one extremity of an open space, hemmed in by the dark wall of the forest, arose a rock, bearing some rude, natural resemblance either to an altar or a pulpit, and surrounded by four blazing pines, their tops aflame, their stems untouched, like candles at an evening meeting."*

John Quinn, a New York lawyer

Lady Murasaki's The Tale of Genji, *a vast chronicle of court life centering on the career of Prince Genji and the women with whom he has associated. It is regarded unreservedly as the greatest single work in Japanese literature, and was translated into English between 1925 and 1933 by Arthur Waley.*

A literary critic once said that before World War II, this book series "was the thing to tuck in your rucksack, or have in your pocket when brought back on a stretcher from the Alps or Spanish Civil War." Recently, the 500-year-old publishing company of the series switched from its little blue-back volumes printed on opaque india paper to paperback. What is the name of the series?

"I have begun on a work which is without precedent whose accomplishment will have no imitator. I propose to set before my fellow-mortals a man in all the truth of nature; and this shall be myself." These famous words come from a figure often identified as the father of European Romanticism. Who is this person, and what is the name of his book?

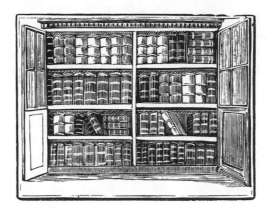

Oxford World Classics, from Oxford University Press. The series was begun at the turn of the century with Jane Eyre *as the first title.*

Jean-Jacques Rousseau. His book is the love-filled, egocentric, exquisitely written, Confessions.

~ Literary Lights ~

◖◗◖◗◖◗————————————————

The first great woman poet of China, she was
captured by a Hun and forced to become his
concubine. Having borne him two sons, she left
both behind when she was ransomed by Ts'ao
Ts'ao, warlord of the Three Kingdoms period.
Who was she?

◖◗◖◗————————————————————

"I have been a writer since 1949. I am self
taught. I have no theories about writing that
might help others. When I write I simply become what I seemingly must become." Who
wrote this and where does it appear?

Ts'ai Yen. Her poem, "18 Verses Sung to a Tatar Reed Whistle," begins:

I was born in a time of peace,
But later the mandate of Heaven
Was withdrawn from the Han Dynasty.

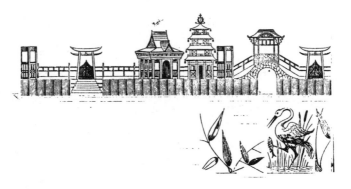

The quotation is from the preface to Welcome to the Monkey House, *by Kurt Vonnegut.*

What character in a 17th-century romantic adventure tries to emulate the fictitious Amadis of Gaul?

Des Esseintes, the decadent hero of J. K. Huysmans' novel *Against the Grain* and Baron Palamède de Charlus of Proust's *Remembrance of Things Past* are each based in part on the same man, the first when he was young, the second during his maturity. Who was this French aristocrat?

What British humorist, long resident in America, performed a daily dozen of Swedish exercises? And what Japanese novelist, after being a 97-pound weakling, made an ethic of bodybuilding?

The character is the intrepid Don Quixote of Cervantes' great novel.

Comte Robert de Montesquiou

P.G. Wodehouse, the creator of Jeeves and Bertie Wooster, was the advocate of a not very rigorous daily dozen. Yukio Mishima, on the other hand, made a cult of bodybuilding, linking it to the warrior class in Japanese society.

The centenary of James Joyce's birth was celebrated in 1982. This great modernist was deeply affected by three women in three different aspects of his life. See if you can fill in the blanks in the following sentences.

a. Without ----, Molly Bloom's ". . . yes I said yes I will Yes," might never have been published.

b. Without ----'s money, Joyce might have starved.

c. Without ---- and her emotional support, Joyce might not have succeeded.

These literary friends made a very odd couple. He was a Brooklyn-born expatriate author who crusaded against convention wherever it dared show itself; she was a French-born Spanish dancer who in one of the many volumes of her diary summed up their differences in the following terms: "[His] definition of human is the one who drinks, forgets, is irresponsible, unfaithful, fallible. Mine is the one who is aware of the feelings of other human beings." Who were they?

a. Sylvia Beach
b. Harriet Shaw Weaver
c. Nora Barnacle

Anais Nin, something of a literary legend, is the diarist. Her great friend was Henry Miller, whose books were admired by George Orwell and T.S. Eliot and whose novel Tropic of Cancer *was the subject of a famous case testing U.S. pornography laws in the early 1960s.*

Guided, he believed, by perpetual visitations
from the spiritual world, this mystical poet and
artist often celebrated the innocence of childhood. The son of a hosier, he met with little public success. Fortunately, his last years were free
of financial hardship because of the generosity
of John Linnell. Can you name the poet and the
title of the poem from which these lines come?

'Drop thy pipe, thy happy pipe,
Sing thy songs of happy cheer,'
So I sung the same again,
While he wept with joy to hear.

William Blake. The poem quoted is "Piping Down the Valleys Wild," also known as "Reeds of Innocence" and "Introduction to Songs of Innocence."

~ Poets and Bards ~

◨◨◨————————————————————

The work of this poet features a cast of characters of the inimitable likes of Slim Greer, Sporting Beasely, Long Gone John, and Crispus Attucks McKoy. Known for his use of folk materials and his deft handling of dialect and natural speech rhythms, he is perhaps most familiar as the author of the following opening stanza: "Swing dat hammer —hunh— /Steady, bo'; / Swing dat hammer—hunh— /Steady, bo'; / Ain't no rush, bebby, / Long way to go." Who is he?

◨◨————————————————————

Described by Wordsworth as "the marvellous boy," this poet ended his career, and life, at 17 by eating arsenic; the paupers' pit at the Shoe Lane Workhouse in London received his remains. Who was he?

Sterling A. Brown, born in Washington in 1901, was first noticed as a poet in 1932 with the publication of Southern Road.

Thomas Chatterton (1752-1770) forged pseudo-medieval verses and later claimed them to be by a 15th-century monk, Thomas Rowley. His scam exposed, he committed suicide.

This daring robber who held up stagecoaches in the 1870s did it alone and on foot with an unloaded shotgun! But if his gun wasn't loaded, his verse (which perhaps he occupied himself with during his stay in prison) certainly was. Here is a sample: "I've labored long and hard for bread/ For honor and for riches/ But on my corns too long you've tread/ You fine-haired Sons of . . . ." Who was this literary marauder and what nom de plume did he go by?

"I am soft sift/In an hourglass—at the wall/Fast, but mined with a motion, a drift/ And it crowds and it combs to the fall. . . " These lines are from an 1876 poem, written in memory of five Franciscan nuns who were drowned in a shipwreck at the mouth of the Thames River. Identify the poet, the poem, and the particular metric in which the poem is written.

Charles E. Boles, alias Black Bart, who seems to have disappeared after being released from jail in 1888.

---

*Gerard Manley Hopkins, himself a Jesuit, com-*posed The Wreck of the Deutschland *in memory of the five drowned nuns. The style—marked by alliteration, assonance, and a strong but ir-regular beat—Hopkins called "sprung rhythm."*

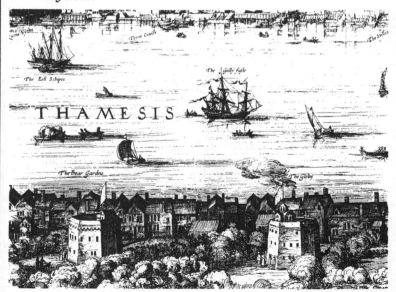

Initiated into Siva worship by an anonymous guru, this Indian poet wandered the world, worshiping Siva in the form of Mallikarjuna, "the lord white as jasmine." One of the poet saints of Virasaivism, the medieval Hindu protestant movement, this poet wrote in Kannada, a Dravidian tongue whose linguistic tradition goes back fifteen centuries:

Like a silkworm weaving her house with love
    from her marrow,
and dying in her body's threads winding tight,
round and round,
I burn,
desiring what the heart desires . . .

Name the poet.

This New Jersey poet was a prodigious writer of essays, short stories, and novels; he was also a full-time doctor. In one of his best known stories he describes a doctor's visit to a young patient who refuses to open her mouth so that he can take a throat culture. Name the writer and his short story.

Mahadeviyakka

William Carlos Williams, the godfather of the Beat, Black Mountain, and the San Francisco poets, wrote "The Use of Force."

A leading figure of the Harlem Renaissance, this poet's prolific literary career spanned 45 years. One of his most famous poems begins:

Droning a drowsy syncopated tune,
Rocking back and forth to a mellow croon,
I heard a Negro play . . .

Who was he?

Snubbed repeatedly by the grande dame who haunts his poetry, this poet finally proposed to her daughter, but she wouldn't have him either, and so he embarked on a marriage about which he quite naturally had some misgivings. His attitudes changed for the better, however, when his new wife, hoping to please him, began an active campaign of automatic writing. He encouraged her, and the voices from the Other World soon gave to him the most intricate symbology since William Blake's. Can you name not only the poet but also the book which presents his esoteric system?

Langston Hughes. Of Harlem, he wrote:

*It's not easy to know what is true for you or me
at twenty-two, my age. But I guess I'm what
I feel and see and hear, Harlem, I hear you:
hear you, hear me—we two—you, me, talk on
    this page.
(I hear New York, too.) Me—Who?*

William Butler Yeats. A Vision *elaborates—
with diagrams—the significance of these
gnomic messages from the spirit world.*

Athletic authors are not so rare as one might imagine. Sophocles was a great wrestler; Ezra Pound studied jiu-jitsu; Kipling golfed; Hemingway boxed. One poet, wanting to emulate the legendary Leander, who swam the Hellespont nightly to be with his beloved Hero, a priestess of Venus, repeated the feat in the company of a Lieutenant Ekenhead of the Royal Navy. Who was this poet whose mode of propulsion was the breast stroke?

Asked by Turgenev to describe his wildest fantasy, this English poet responded "To ravish St. Genevieve during her most ardent ecstasy of prayer — but in addition, with her secret consent." Obsessed with Eton's infamous flogging block, he was rescued from death by the critic, poet, and novelist Walter Theodore Watts-Dunton, and spent the rest of his life at his estate. Who was he?

Lord Byron, who though dashingly handsome and always the ladies' favorite, is said to have been obsessed with his prowess. That he was born with a clubfoot may have had something to do with it.

Algernon Swinburne, author of the deliciously decadent poem "Dolores"—Our Lady of Pain. Max Beerbohm's celebrated essay "No. 2, the Pines" describes a visit to Swinburne and Watts-Dunton.

Not only there
Does he see this sight,
But everywhere
In his brain—day, night,
As if on the air. . . .

Considered to be the last "Grand Old Man" of
English letters, this novelist and poet was buried
in Westminster Abbey, but his heart found its
final resting place in Dorset. His marital history
has perplexed biographers; unkind to his first
wife while she lived, he fell passionately back in
love with his memories of her as a girl after she
died—and after he had married his second wife.
Who was he? And name the poem from which
the above lines come.

Even great American poets have served as government employees in Washington. During the
Civil War era, one such poet completed the
fourth and fifth editions of a book of poetry
while working as a government clerk and as a
volunteer nurse in nearby military hospitals.
Who was the poet and what was the title of the
book?

*Thomas Hardy. His novels are read in high
school, but his poetry, less well known, has influenced such English poets as W.H. Auden.
The verses quoted come from "The Phantom
Horsewoman."*

---

*Walt Whitman, who originally went to Wash-
ington just before Christmas 1862 to find his
brother, George, who had been reported wound-
ed. Whitman stayed with his brother in camp
and when he returned to Washington, rented a
small room, found a job as copyist in the Army
paymaster's office, and began visiting Brooklyn
soldiers in the hospitals. Whitman's experiences in the hospitals and at the front led him
to proclaim that "The Real War Will Never Get
in the Books," but his collection* Drum-Taps
*(1865) is largely concerned with just this aim.
Whitman's most famous war poem is of course
"When Lilacs Last in the Dooryard Bloom'd," a
poem written on the occasion of Lincoln's assassination.*

To have gathered from the air a live tradition
Or from a fine old eye the unconquered flame
This is not vanity.
Here error is all in the not done,
All in the diffidence that faltered.

The poet who wrote these lines spent 13 years in
federal custody at St. Elizabeths Hospital in
Washington, D.C. Who was he?

Father of three illegitimate daughters, all named
Elizabeth and each from a different mother, this
poet of legendary passion gave his brother some
very different advice: "To have a woman to lye
with as one pleases, without running any risk of
cursed expense of bastards. . . . These are
solid views of matrimony." He however did not
practice what he preached.

But my downcast eye by chance did spy
What made my lips to water,
Those limbs so clean where I, between,
Commenc'd a Fornicator.

Who was he?

*These lines are Ezra Pound's and are taken
from the* Pisan Cantos, *written from the
memory of the deprivations and humiliations
he suffered during the months of his imprison-
ment in an open air cage in Italy. The poet had
been taken into custody because of the radio
broadcasts he delivered during the war in which
he denounced President Roosevelt and advo-
cated various activities of Mussolini as condu-
cive to a new society no longer based on money
grubbing (views he later retracted). Pound was
to stand trial for treason in the States in 1945,
but his case was suspended when the court, ac-
cepting the report of a panel of psychiatrists,
found Pound "insane and mentally unfit for
trial." Until the charge of treason was dropped
in 1958, Pound was a patient in St. Elizabeths
Hospital, where, set up in a private room, he
worked on the* Cantos *and was visited by his devoted wife and many admirers, among them
T.S. Eliot, Archibald MacLeish and Robert
Lowell.*

---

*Robert Burns, whose bawdy Caledonian verse
can still bring a blush to an innocent's cheek*

■_____

This poet, influential at court through his association with John of Gaunt and his family, also wrote some of the finest poetry in English:

Whan that Aprille with hise shoures sote
The droghte of March hath perced to the rote,
And bathed every veyne in swich licour,
Of which vertu engendred is the flour. . . .

Who was he, and from what work do these lines come?

■■_____

Best known for his crafty flirtations with a certain coy mistress and his penchant for the cool green shade of bowered gardens, this poet at one time served as the assistant to a poet greater than himself and wrote the following lines about his master's greatest work:

When I beheld the poet blind, yet bold,
In slender book his vast design unfold. . . .

Who was the poet and whom did he serve?

The poet Geoffrey Chaucer (circa 1343-1400) was born into a wine merchant's family. He was first introduced to the noble circle he later became identified with when he served as a page in the household of Lionel of Antwerp, brother of John of Gaunt. The verses quoted from are the famous opening lines of The Canterbury Tales.

Andrew Marvell, beloved for his "To His Coy Mistress," worked for John Milton, who was then the Latin secretary to the government of Commonwealth England and blind, in need of a secretary.

~ Literary Lodgings ~

📖_____

Poet Felicia Hemans (1793-1835) wrote about
"the stately homes" and "the cottage homes of
England." The following may be one or the
other or something in between. Name their best-
known inhabitants:

a. The Pines
b. Greenway
c. Dove Cottage
d. Gad's Hill Place

The Pines (Algernon Swinburne)
Greenway (Agatha Christie)
Dove Cottage (William Wordsworth)
Gad's Hill Place (Charles Dickens)

❚❚_____

One of the most endearing and well-known characters in English literature lodged in the house of this man, who confided to his lodger the sum of his worldly philosophy:

"Annual income twenty pounds; annual expenditure nineteen, nineteen, six—result happiness. Annual income twenty pounds. Annual expenditure twenty pounds nought six—result misery."

Who was this man, and who was his young boarder?

❚❚_____

Tony Last lives at a suitably removed distance from London in an old Gothic mansion, where he tries to carry on the tradition of the English gentleman. Though the house and grounds are unappreciated by nearly everyone—it is too large, too cold, its rambling design seems without plan, its old battlements seem somewhat absurd against the modern sky, it is in grave disrepair—it is Last's most cherished dream to restore it to its past feudal glory. This dream never materializes, for he becomes an explorer in Brazil and is captured by a mad old man who forces him to read Dickens aloud day and night. What is the name of the house?

The man who espoused this philosophy was Mr. Micawber, David Copperfield's landlord, in Dickens' novel.

Hetton Abbey (Evelyn Waugh, A Handful of Dust)

◖◖◖————————————————

This author took it upon himself to defend himself and others of the writing trade against the charge that dividing books into chapters was just another way of padding, of adding length and thus profit to the finished product. He did so in the following terms:

"But in reality the case is otherwise, and in this, as well as all other instances, we consult the advantage of our reader, not our own; and indeed many notable uses arise to him from this method; for, first, those little spaces between our chapters may be looked upon as an inn or resting-place where he may stop and take a glass, or any other refreshment, as it pleases him. Nay, our fine readers will, perhaps, be scarce able to travel farther than through one of them in a day. As to those vacant pages which are placed between . . . they are to be regarded as those stages, where in long journeys, the traveller stays some time to repose himself, and consider of what he hath seen in parts he hath already passed through."

Who is this author and what is the book the above quote pads?

Henry Fielding, Joseph Andrews

Whose midnight musings are we privy to here?

"In what ultimate ambition had all concurrent and consecutive ambitions now coalesced?

Not to inherit by right of primogeniture, gravelkind or borough English, or possess in perpetuity and extensive demesne of a sufficient number of acres, roods and perches, statute land measure (valuation £42), of grazing turbary surrounding a baronial hall with gatelodge and carriage drive nor, on the other hand, a terracehouse or semidetached villa, described as *Rus in Urbe* or *Qui si Sana*, but to purchase by private treaty in fee simple a thatched bungalowshaped 2 storey dwelling-house of southerly aspect, surmounted by vane and lightning conductor, connected with the earth, with porch covered by parasitic plants (ivy or Virginia creeper), halldoor, olive green, with smart carriage finish and neat doorbrasses, stucco front with gilt tracery at eaves and gable, rising, if possible upon a gentle eminence with agreeable prospect. . . ."

Leopold Bloom's in James Joyce's Ulysses

To whom do the following famous American cabins belong?

a. "The cabin. . . was a small log building, close adjoining to 'the house,' as the Negro 'par exellence' designates his master's dwelling. In front it had a neat gardenpatch, where, every summer, strawberries, raspberries, and a variety of fruits and vegetables, flourished under careful tending. The whole front of it was covered by a large scarlet bignonia and a native multiflora rose, which, entwisting and interlacing, left scarce a vestige of the rough logs to be seen."

b. "This was an airy and unplastered cabin, fit to entertain a travelling god, and where a goddess might trail her garments."

c. "There warn't a window to it big enough for a dog to get through. I couldn't get up the chimbly; it was too narrow. The door was thick, solid oak slabs."

a. Uncle Tom
b. Thoreau
c. Huck Finn

~ What's in a Name? ~

What American children's writer used the
pseudonym Edith Van Dyne?

Jean Plaidy, Philippa Carr and Victoria Holt are
all pseudonyms of romantic suspense novelists.
What are their real names?

What famous author defended the rights of his
countrymen under the pen name of Malachi
Malagrowther?

L. Frank Baum, the author of The Wizard *of Oz and its 13 sequels, wrote about 60 books during his life, about half of which were stories for girls written under the pseudonym Edith Van Dyne. Possessing an imagination that could transform the close-at-hand into the marvelous, Baum is reported to have found the name for his magical kingdom on his set of file cabinets: they read A—N and O—Z.*

All three are pseudonyms for the British novelist Eleanor Hibbert, who also publishes under the pen names Elbur Ford, Kathleen Kellow and Ellalice Tate. Hibbert has published in the neighborhood of 200 books. She has said, "I think people want a good story and this I give them."

Malachi Malagrowther was the pen name with which Sir Walter Scott signed three letters in 1826, on the question of the Scottish paper currency, to the Edinburgh Weekly Journal. *Scott, who also published his fabulously popular Waverly novels anonymously, was called "The Great Unknown" by his publisher and "The Wizard of the North" by his readers.*

📖📖————————————————————

What do these three pseudonymous writers have in common?

George Eliot
James Tiptree, Jr.
Currer Bell

📖📖📖————————————————————

Who was the author who named himself after a bandit?

They were all female.

American poet Cincinnatus Hiner Miller used the pseudonym Joaquin Miller because his early writings defended the Mexican bandit Joaquin Murietta.

The
∽ Children's Hour ∽

📖📖📖——————————————————————

"I'm tired of books, tired of books," said
Jack
"I long for meadows green,
And woods where shadowy violets
Nod their cool leaves between."

What poet, who identified often with young
readers, wrote these anti-bookish lines? And in
what poem?

📖📖📖——————————————————————

What little boy has some pretty amazing adventures with a big purple crayon? Who created
him?

Walter de la Mare in "The Bookworm"

Harold was created by Crockett Johnson in
Harold and the Purple Crayon.

■———————————————————————————

Eight-year-old Henry Huggins lives on Klickitat
Street in Portland, Oregon, along with his
friends Beezus and Ramona, as well as his ever-
growing family of guppies. In the same city,
Ellen Tebbets resides in the Tillamook Street
neighborhood where she does battle with her
enemy, Otis Spofford. And, of course, who could
ever forget that daring little mouse, Ralph, who
zips about on a toy motorcycle? Who created
these wonderful characters?

■———————————————————————————

What toy becomes truly "real" because of a little
boy's love and some assistance from the nursery
fairy?

■■———————————————————————————

A famous spy novelist once wrote a children's
story about a most unusual car. What was its
name and who dreamed it up?

Beverly Cleary is the author of more than a score of books for children, which have sold 3.4 million copies since Henry Huggins *was first published in 1950.*

The rabbit, star of The Velveteen Rabbit: Or How Toys Become Real *by Margery Williams*

Ian Fleming wrote a story about a flying car called Chitty Chitty Bang Bang, *which was subsequently made into a highly successful movie starring Dick Van Dyke and Sally Ann Howes. Roald Dahl, author of* Charlie and the Chocolate Factory, *helped write the screenplay.*

One of the most beloved creatures of a lifetime is the teddy bear. Who created the following stuffed characters?

Aloysius
Winnie-the-Pooh
Paddington
Rupert Bear
Boots, Slippers and Socks

Evelyn Waugh created Aloysius, who was trailed about Oxford by young Sebastian Marchmain, in Brideshead Revisited.

A.A. Milne wrote about Winnie-the-Pooh, in real life a stuffed bear belonging to his son Christopher Robin.

Englishman Michael Bond is the author of 14 books about Paddington Bear, who acquired his name when he met the Brown family in London's Paddington Station. He himself was a stowaway from darkest Peru.

Mary Tourtel, collaborating with her husband, first introduced Rupert Bear in a story called The Adventures of a Little Lost Bear, *published, as a comic strip, in 1920 in the* Daily Express *of London. Rupert has enjoyed public life ever since. In 1935 Mary Tourtel passed the job of chronicling this winning little bear's adventures over to A.E. Bestall.*

Margaret J. Baker is the imagination behind The Shoeshop Bears, *the story of Boots, Slippers and Socks. These three bears inhabit Mr. Shoehorn's shoe store, and are described in his stock list as "Three stuffed toy bears, large, medium, and small, for the comfort, amusement, and edification of juvenile customers during the fitting of their footwear." But they are decidedly more than stuffed.*

📖‾‾‾‾‾‾‾‾‾‾‾‾‾‾‾‾‾‾‾‾‾‾‾‾‾‾‾‾‾‾

By 1975, this book had sold almost 2 million
copies, making it the best-selling children's book
of the 20th century. What is the title of this best
seller which revolves around food?

📖📖‾‾‾‾‾‾‾‾‾‾‾‾‾‾‾‾‾‾‾‾‾‾‾‾‾

Name the Dover mouse who swam across the
English Channel atop a mackerel, flew back with
the help of a seagull, and got home in time for
fish and chips.

📖📖‾‾‾‾‾‾‾‾‾‾‾‾‾‾‾‾‾‾‾‾‾‾‾‾‾

A grandniece of Mark Twain wrote a popular
novel for young people. The story portrays the
coming of age of a spunky female orphan. Who
was she? Who gave her life in what book?

Green Eggs and Ham *by Dr. Seuss continues to sell over 100,000 copies a year.*

Aktil, of Aktil's Big Swim *by Inga Moore*

The girl from the John Grier Asylum had the unlikely name of Jerusha Abbott, picked for her from the phone book and a tombstone. Her letters to an unknown benefactor form the novel Daddy-Long-Legs *by Jean Webster.*

~ Love of Learning ~

▌▌▌————————————————————————

"There exists one book, which, to my taste, furnishes the happiest treatise of natural education. What then is this marvelous book? Is it Aristotle? Is it Pliny, is it Buffon? No, it is -------." Thus spoke a famous 18th-century philosopher. Who was he, and what book does he have in mind?

▌————————————————————————————

This early American was self-taught in the classroom of experience, with the occasional help of a furtively borrowed book. Later in life, his position in the world well secured, he helped establish a circulating library and a school that was to become the University of Pennsylvania.

Rousseau, in his educational romance, Emile, ou L'Education *(1762) in which the author describes the bringing up of a boy according to what are called the principles of nature, was referring to* Robinson Crusoe, *written by Daniel Defoe and published a half a century earlier in 1719.*

Benjamin Franklin, a self-made man of myriad talents, helped to establish, among his many other contributions as statesman, printer, scientist and writer, the Academy for the Education of Youth (1751), the forerunner to the University of Pennsylvania. Along similar lines, in 1727 he formed the "Junto," a debating club which was to become the American Philosophical Society (1743).

▯▯————————————————————

A shy bachelor who spent his life as a tutor of
classics at Oxford, this 19th-century aestheti-
cian and novelist was surprised and even
alarmed by the impact made by his books on
young readers. Oscar Wilde and George Moore
found his work, in its quiet way, more subversive
than the head-on attacks against traditional
Victorianism made by Swinburne or Samuel
Butler. Instead of echoing the call to duty and
social responsibility of his conservative contemporaries, he reminded his readers that life passes
quickly and that our only responsibility is to
enjoy fully "this short day of frost and sun," to
relish its sensations, especially those provoked
by works of art. Who was this advocate of Art
for Art's sake?

▯————————————————————

A member of the Harvard faculty at the turn of
the century, this Spanish-born philosopher and
poet is probably best known for his quote:
"Those who cannot remember the past are condemned to repeat it."

Walter Pater (1839-94), a fellow of Brasenose College, Oxford, first made his name with Studies in the History of the Renaissance *(1873). He was associated with the Pre-Raphaelites.*

George Santayana (1863-1952), who penned this remark in The Life of Reason, *taught at Harvard from 1907 to 1912. Among his students there were: Conrad Aiken, Robert Benchley, Felix Frankfurter, Walter Lippmann, and T.S. Eliot.*

■ ————————————————

This famous woman's college was scandalized by an alumna who based one of her best known novels on her experiences there. In addition to being a novelist, she had reviewed plays for *Partisan Review,* and had been married to a leading man of letters. Name the college, the novel based on it, its author, and her literary spouse.

▮▮ ————————————————

Universities have often been settings for fiction. One novel, set at Oxford in the early 1900s, tells of a bewitching young woman and her effect on the male students—they commit suicide for love of her. Who is the eponymous heroine of this satire?

▮▮ ————————————————

Philip Roth, John Gunther and Saul Bellow all have a common academic stomping ground. Where is it?

▮▮▮ ————————————————

"The justification for a university is that it preserves the connection between knowledge and the zest of life, by uniting the young and the old in the imaginative consideration of learning," was the sentiment expressed by what famous educator?

Vassar College was the institution upon which Mary McCarthy, a 1933 graduate, based her novel The Group *(1963). McCarthy had been married to Edmund Wilson.*

Zuleika Dobson, from the novel by Max Beerbohm published in 1911

The University of Chicago: Philip Roth received his M.A. in English Literature at Chicago in 1955 after attending Bucknell University; John Gunther graduated from the Chicago class of 1922; Saul Bellow studied for a time at Chicago but transferred to Northwestern where he took a degree in 1937 in anthropology and sociology.

Alfred North Whitehead, who taught both at England's Imperial College of Science and Technology and at Harvard University, wrote about the justification of a university in his book The Aims of Education *(1929).*

∽ Furred, Finny ∽ and Feathered Friends

The titles of the following books become complete when filled in with the name of an animal. Identify their authors as well:

1. *The Red -----*
2. *------ Cradle*
3. *The Celebrated Jumping------ of Calaveras County*

Can you name the literary animals, and their creator, who munched on the following feast?

They dined on mince, and slices of quince, Which they ate with a runcible spoon.

1. The Red Pony, *by John Steinbeck*
2. Cat's Cradle, *by Kurt Vonnegut*
3. The Celebrated Jumping Frog of Calaveras County, *by Mark Twain*

According to Edward Lear, the Owl and the Pussy Cat, in the poem by the same name (published in 1871), dined on this special feast.

📖————————————————————

To whom did "Captain Flint" belong and what
was he?

📖📖📖————————————————————

This bon vivant, scholar and poet, who was committed to an insane asylum for nearly seven
years for praying in the streets, had as his sole
companion during confinement a cat to whom
he wrote the following verses:

For I will consider my Cat Jeoffry.
For he is the servant of the Living God, duly and
    daily serving him.
For at the first glance of the glory of God in the
    East he worships in his way.
For this is done by wreathing his body seven
    times round with elegant quickness

📖📖————————————————————

Herman Melville's *Moby Dick* is probably the
best known of the New England "whale tales."
Some have claimed that Melville owed his inspi-
ration for the famous yarn to an equally famous
New England author. Who was this alleged
source?

117

Captain Flint was the parrot belonging to Long John Silver in Treasure Island *(1883), by Robert Louis Stevenson.*

Christopher Smart (1722–71), a poet chiefly remembered for his "Song to David" (1763), died in a debtor's prison.

Nathaniel Hawthorne was a close friend, and neighbor, of Melville's in Lenox, Massachusetts, and his allegorical tales of the struggle between good and evil are known to have made a profound impression on Melville as well as many other American writers.

"It's very, very funny,
'Cause *I know* I had some honey;
'Cause it had a label on,
    Saying HUNNY.

A goloptious full-up pot too,
And I don't know where it's got to,
No, I don't know where it's gone—
    Well, it's funny."

What hungry character in a 1920s children's
book murmured this to himself? Who had eaten
most of the honey?

When Frank J. Lieverman whimsically introduced "Gertrude the Kangeroo" as the colophon
for the first paperback publishing company in
1939, he probably didn't realize that the mar-
supial he had named after his mother-in-law
would become part of a billion-dollar international industry. What is the name of the mass-
market publishing house to which "Gertrude"
still belongs?

Winnie-the-Pooh is guilty on both counts.

Pocket Books Inc.

～ For Whom ～ the Bell Tolls

🔖🔖🔖_____

What famous American writer foretold his own suicide in a semi-autobiographical novel?

🔖🔖_____

What defender of Ireland is buried under the following epitaph (translated from the Latin): "He has gone where savage indignation can tear his heart no more"?

🔖🔖_____

Who wrote his own epitaph: "Here lies one whose name was writ in water," and in what cemetery was he buried?

Jack London in Martin Eden *(1909) tells the story of a writer who is first unsuccessful and rejected, and later successful and lionized by the hypocrites who had initially turned their backs on him.*

Jonathan Swift (1667-1745) is buried in St. Patrick's Cathedral, Dublin, under the epitaph (which in Latin reads) "ubi saeva indignatio ulterius cor lacerare nequit." Swift, as dean of St. Patrick's, and as a writer (probably best known today for Gulliver's Travels*) vented his spleen frequently in print against the oppression suffered by Ireland.*

The English poet John Keats (1795-1821) died of tuberculosis in Rome and was buried in the Protestant Cemetery there.

An American journalist and writer known for his ambitious portraits of sometimes entire continents was moved, mid-career, to turn away from his public subjects to write about a very private one, the tragic death of his son from a brain tumor. Name this author and the title of his book, which was taken from a sonnet written by Donne?

Name the principal characters in the following works who committed suicide:

a. *The Sound and the Fury*
b. *Death of a Salesman*
c. *Nicholas Nickleby*
d. *Jude the Obscure*
e. *Sister Carrie*
f. *The Brothers Karamazov*

What author documented the gruesome murder of a peaceable farm family near Holcomb, Kansas, the Clutters, and the ensuing flight of the killers into Mexico and back into the States where they were arrested in Kansas—proving the saying that the criminal always returns to the scene of the crime?

John Gunther, Death Be Not Proud

---

a. Quentin Compson
b. Willy Loman
c. Ralph Nickleby
d. Jude's son, also called Jude or Little Father Time
e. George Hurstwood
f. Smerdyakov

Truman Capote; the book was In Cold Blood

Master of the murmuring courts
  Where the shapes of sleep convene!—
Lo! my spirit here exhorts
  All the powers of thy demesne
  For their aid to woo my queen.
    What reports
Yield thy jealous courts unseen?

This is the first stanza of a long poem written by a member of the so-called "fleshly school of poetry." Its content is mystical, but its publication history is even stranger. In 1870 it was taken from a grave in which it had lain, with other manuscripts, for seven years. The grave was that of the poet's wife, and he had placed the poems there in honor of her whom he had courted 10 years before their brief marriage ended with her death. The decision to retrieve the poems was not an easy one, and yet the manuscript was the only complete copy of this poet's early, much labored work. The grave was opened and the coffin exhumed at night by the light of a fire, and the manuscript published not long after. Name the poet, and the title of the poem quoted from above.

Dante Gabriel Rossetti, Love's Nocturne

∾ Food for Thought ∾

▌◖▌

In 1825 this French lawyer wrote a famous book about food. He holds the distinction of having a dessert named after him. Can you name the man, the book, and the sweet which bears his name?

▌

According to George Bernard Shaw, "There is no love sincerer than the love of food." Can you fill in the missing edibles?

1. Proust ate a ------with a cup of tisane.
2. Persephone munched on some seeds from a --------.
3. For his breakfast, Leopold Bloom cooked up a -------.

Anthelme Brillat-Savarin wrote La Physiologie du goût *translated into English in 1925 as* The Physiology of Taste. *The dessert named after him is the Savarin, a sweet and rich yeast cake usually soaked with rum.*

---

1. Proust ate a madeleine with a cup of tisane.
2. Persephone munched on some seeds from a pomegranate.
3. For his breakfast Leopold Bloom cooked up a kidney.

Americans' eating habits have made us into weight-watching, calorie-counting fanatics. As a result, books such as *The Complete Scarsdale Medical Diet,* by Herman Tarnower and *Richard Simmons Never-Say-Diet Book* have satisfied publishers' commercial appetites by becoming best sellers. This, however, is not a recent phenomenon. In the '20s one book dedicated to physical well-being was on the best-seller list for five years, and was number one in 1924 and 1925. Name the book and the author.

Can you name these writers dining out at Magny's in Paris? Here's some help.

1. One had a love affair with the poet Louise Colet.
2. Another founded an Academy to foster fiction.
3. A third seduced Victor Hugo's wife.
4. His novel offended the revolutionaries and the reactionaries of Imperial Russia.

Lulu Hunt Peters wrote Diet and Health.

Gustave Flaubert, Edmond de Goncourt, Charles Sainte-Beuve, and Ivan Turgenev are dining out at Magny's.

◨————————————————————————

What maiden in a 19th-century English romance is now the name of a shortbread cookie?

◨◨◨————————————————————————

"Egg beaters whirl, spoons spin round in bowls of butter and sugar, vanilla sweetens the air, ginger spices it; melting, nose-tingling odors saturate the kitchen . . . "

Just add some pecans, whiskey, and a few other ingredients for the recipe that became a yearly ritual for this author and his elderly cousin in his touching autobiographical Christmas memoir. What is the treat and who is the author?

Lorna Doone, the heroine of a novel by the same name, written by R.D. Blackmore and published in 1869. The story is set in the wilds of England's Exmoor during the times of Charles II and James II.

Truman Capote's recipe for fruitcake

❧ Stage and Screen ❧

📖————————————————————————

A central character in the popular television series M★A★S★H assumed the name of an Indian character in one of America's most famous 19th-century novels. Identify M★A★S★H's character, the Indian whose name he took, and the novel in which he appeared.

📖————————————————————————

Francis Ford Coppola's film *Apocalypse Now* follows the essential story line of what 20th-century literary classic?

📖————————————————————————

"Beware the Ides of March," cries a soothsayer to a Roman general in a famous play. To whom was the warning given, in what play, and what are the ides of March?

The M★A★S★H character Franklin Pierce adopted the name "Hawkeye," taken from one of several names used by Natty Bumppo in James Fenimore Cooper's five novels known collectively as The Leatherstocking Tales. *Natty Bumppo is known as Hawkeye in* The Last of the Mohicans *(1826). Elsewhere in Cooper's work he is known by other names such as: Leatherstocking, Pathfinder and Deerslayer.*

Heart of Darkness *by Joseph Conrad*

The warning was given to Julius Caesar in the play of the same name by William Shakespeare. According to the ancient Roman calendar, the ides of March were the 15th day of March

What famous writers worked on the screenplays of the following films?:

a. *To Have and Have Not*
b. *Dead End*
c. *Gone With the Wind*
d. *Pride and Prejudice*
e. *Beat the Devil*
f. *The African Queen*
g. *The Big Sleep*

🔖

This book, which was first a movie and includes many brilliant stills from the film, tells the story of young Pascal who is befriended by a magic balloon. When a group of toughs chase him through the streets of Paris, all the escaped balloons of the city come to his rescue.

🔖🔖🔖

The movie *Rachel, Rachel* starring Joanne Woodward and directed by her husband Paul Newman, in his directorial debut, was based on a prize-winning Canadian novel. Can you name the novel and its author?

To Have and Have Not *(1945) William Faulkner*
Dead End *(1937) Lillian Hellman*
Gone With the Wind *(1939) F. Scott Fitzgerald*
Pride and Prejudice *(1940) Aldous Huxley*
Beat the Devil *(1953) Truman Capote*
The African Queen *(1951) James Agee*
The Big Sleep *(1946) William Faulkner*

The film The Red Balloon, *was produced and directed by Albert Lamorisse. It won rave reviews from critics and, among other awards, Hollywood's coveted Oscar—the Motion Picture Academy Award for the best original screenplay of 1956. The book, memorable for the color photographs taken from the movie, was published in the same year.*

Rachel, Rachel *was based on Margaret Laurence's* A Jest of God *which won the Governor General's award in 1967.*

Known as "Public Lover No. 1" because of some indiscreet entries in Mary Astor's diary, this American playwright collaborated with the Marx Brothers on three of their most successful movies. A famed wit of the Algonquin Round Table, he once remarked, "The trouble with incest is that it gets you involved with relatives." Who was he?

Her heart-rending tale is that of a Wessex lass who goes to the greenwood and returns a maid no more. She bears a child christened Sorrow, slays her seducer, and spends her last night of freedom upon a sacrificial altar at Stonehenge with a man named Angel. For her creator, she was "a Pure Woman ... more sinned against than sinning." For Roman Polanski, she was the subject of a film. Who was she?

What do the following have in common? *A Breath of Air,* by the popular British novelist Rumer Godden, and *Forbidden Planet,* a 1956 science-fiction film starring Walter Pidgeon and Anne Francis?

George S. Kaufman, who's perhaps best known for his play, You Can't Take It With You, *written with Moss Hart in 1936*

Tess Durbeyfield, from the novel Tess of the d'Urbervilles *(1891) by Thomas Hardy*

They are both updated versions of Shakespeare's play The Tempest.

~ Poetic Puzzles ~

◖◗◖◗◖◗_____

Founded and spearheaded by one of the 20th century's greatest poets and poetic mentors, this literary movement degenerated into what its founder called "Amygism" under the influence of latecomers such as Amy Lowell. Still, its prescription led to such famous poems as "In a Station of the Metro": "The apparition of these faces in the crowd;/ Petals on a wet, black bough." Name the poet and the movement.

◖◗◖◗◖◗_____

What great poet, dissatisfied with St. John's mystical opening, "In the beginning was the Word," revised it to read "In the beginning was the Deed"?

Early in his career Ezra Pound founded, in large part, the literary movement called Imagism.

Goethe in Faust

◨◨————————————————————————

Literature, like any other activity, has its disagreements: "All good poetry is the spontaneous overflow of powerful feelings . . . " but "Poetry is not a turning loose of emotion, but an escape from emotion." Name the proponents of these contradictory theories.

◨◨◨————————————————————————

Japanese literature is filled with poetry anthologies. In the middle of the 8th century, members of the court aristocracy put together the most famous and revered anthology, one which contains over 4,500 poems. What is it called in Japanese—and in English?

◨————————————————————————

Thomas Hardy's *Far from the Madding Crowd* is a rich and fascinating portrait of life in rural 19th-century England. In which poem, by an 18th-century English poet, did Hardy discover the title for his novel?

William Wordsworth wrote the first in his famous preface to Lyrical Ballads. *T.S. Eliot, in the essays collected in* The Sacred Wood, *put forward a more classical view of poetry.*

Manyoshu. *There are several English translations, including* Collection of 10,000 Leaves, Collection for a Myriad Age, *and* Collection of a Myriad Leaves.

"Elegy Written in a Country Churchyard," by Thomas Gray. "Far from the madding crowd's ignoble strife,/Their sober wishes never learned to stray;/Along the cool sequestered vale of life/ They kept the noiseless tenor of their way."

◨◨◨————————————————

Prisons and visions presented
with rare descriptions
corresponding exactly to those
of Alcatraz and Rose

This is a verse from a poem read in court during
the obscenity trial concerning a controversial
Beat novel. Identify the poet, his poem, and the
novel on trial.

*Allen Ginsberg read "On Burroughs' Work"
during the trial involving William Burroughs'*
Naked Lunch, *a novel in large part about addiction to "junk," or heroin.*

~ Dr. Watson ~
and Company

▐▌▐▌▐▌——————————————————————

Many authors in the mystery and suspense genre have been eminent under other identities. Can you give two names for each of the following personages: A British poet laureate, an American art historian and critic, and an American novelist and essayist?

▐▌▐▌▐▌——————————————————————

Name the creators of the following detectives modeled after Sherlock Holmes:

Solar Pons
Mr. Mycroft
Schlock Homes

145

Cecil Day-Lewis wrote mysteries under the name Nicholas Blake. His detective Nigel Strangeways was originally based on his friend and fellow poet W.H. Auden. John Canaday, former art critic for The New York Times, *wrote several mysteries early in his career under the name Matthew Head. Gore Vidal has written mysteries as Edgar Box.*

August Derleth deliberately imitated the Holmes saga in his many stories of Solar Pons. H.F. Heard pictures the Master (or some think his brother, Mycroft) in retirement under the name Mr. Mycroft. Robert L. Fish wrote some of the best comic, pun-filled send-ups in his series in Ellery Queen's Mystery Magazine *devoted to the adventures of the incredible Schlock Homes.*

📖_____

They met when she was a defendant in the dock. She wrote detective stories; he was a detective. She was accused of murder—he found evidence to absolve her of guilt. She was too sensible and protective of her independence to accept his rash marriage proposal. Two books later they finally wed. Unfortunately, a corpse joined them on their honeymoon. Can you name these lovers and the particular day of the unspecified year they tied the knot?

📖_____

In fiction, detectives often come in pairs. Besides Holmes and Watson, there are the following detective teams. Can you identify them?

a. They keep Siamese cats and live in New York's Greenwich Village.
b. She weighs over 200 pounds and he is a pipsqueak.
c. One is the "brains," while the other is the "legs."

On the 8th of October Lord Peter Wimsey wed Harriet Vane. They met in Strong Poison, *courted—stormily—in* Gaudy Night *and finally tied the knot in* Busman's Honeymoon. *Dorothy Sayers created these lovers of literary allusion who kept bumping into death.*

---

a. Pamela and Jerry North, the brain-couple of Frances and Richard Lockridge

b. Erle Stanley Gardner created the hefty Bertha Cool and the fast-talking Donald Lam.

c. Rex Stout's Nero Wolfe almost never leaves his New York brownstone; instead Archie Goodwin does the on-the-spot investigating, leaving Wolfe to make the final deductions.

❏❏ _____

What 18th-century man of letters published a
novel which many scholars consider to have
been the first mystery, and what was its title? In
addition, who was his daughter, author of a
seminal "horror" story?

❏❏ _____

What notable Belgian crime writer once composed a novel in 24 hours while suspended in a
cage in a busy department store?

❏❏ _____

Name the tour-de-force 20th-century English
suspense novel which takes its title from a
candy.

❏❏❏ _____

Which two mystery writers graduated from Harvard prior to World War II, worked briefly for
Boston newspapers, and created inscrutable
sleuths made famous by the movies?

Social philosopher William Godwin wrote Things as They Are, or The Adventures of Caleb Williams. *His daughter, Mary Godwin Shelley, thought up the Godwinian Gothic,* Frankenstein.

———————————

Georges Simenon, the man behind Inspector Maigret

———————————

Brighton Rock, *by Graham Greene, with its famous proto-punk gang leader, Pinkie*

———————————

Earl Derr Biggers created Charlie Chan; John P. Marquand thought up Mr. Moto.

∽ Republic ∽
of Letters

❧

Two accounts of expeditions—one a surveying trip along the border of Virginia and North Carolina, and one a journey to the mouth of the Columbia River and back—have become early classics of our history and literature. Titles and authors, please.

In 1728 William Byrd, the son of a wealthy Virginia planter and a man of considerable wit and learning—his library of 4,000 volumes was reputedly the largest in the English colonies—was commissioned to survey the much disputed boundary line between Virginia and North Carolina. The diary which he kept on this trip served as the source for **The History of the Dividing Line Between Virginia and North Carolina,** *a book that, although it was not published until 1841, was circulated among his European friends and came to be known later by Thomas Jefferson.*

Even before Jefferson had made his famous Louisiana Purchase, he appointed his secretary, Meriwether Lewis, to command an exploring party, and Lewis chose his Army friend William Clark to share its leadership. With the goal of finding an inland route to the Pacific, they and their party of about 40 set out from St. Louis in the winter of 1803-4; more than two years later, in September 1806, they arrived back in St. Louis, having accomplished all they had set out to do and more. The official journal in two volumes was published in 1814; the definitive edition of eight volumes was finally completed and published in 1904-5.

Many American writers have illuminated the national character through tales of baseball and the eternal diamond. Born in Michigan, this author wrote "You Know Me, Al: A Busher's Letters" about a novice among professionals. Who was he?

American letters has so far produced only one 200-pound, cigar-smoking, salty author who could usually be seen accompanied by packs of dogs. Who was she?

Her diary numbered 69 volumes and 35,000 handwritten pages. Spanish, she claimed, was the language of her ancestors, French that of her heart, and English that of her intellect. A model for the top illustrators of her day, she wrote elegant erotica for a dollar a page—as well as more experimental novels. Who was she?

Ring Lardner—author of some of the funniest, and most bitter, stories in American literature

---

Amy Lowell (1847-1925) was a member of the old and distinguished Lowell family of New England, and in her own right was a respected poet, critic and biographer. She was eccentric to a fault. Ezra Pound complained that she had converted "Imagism" (a poetic movement that Pound had spearheaded) into "Amygism."

Anais Nin, the 20th century's answer to Samuel Pepys, condensed her 69 personal volumes into seven for publication. They cover the years 1931 to 1974.

◖◗◖◗◖◗————————————————

The following men were all publishers of a type
of book that became a best seller in colonial
America and is still popular today. What is the
type of book? And what are the titles of the
early editions written by the following distinguished colonists?

a. Robert Bailey Thomas
b. James Franklin
c. Benjamin Franklin

◖◗◖◗◖◗————————————————

Declaring he wished to be a "writer like my great
granddaddy," this Nobel Prize winner described
his ancestors in several novels of southern life
featuring the Sartoris and Snopes families.
Name both the famous novelist and his "granddaddy," then give the title of the older one's
most famous work.

a. The Old Farmer's Almanack
b. The Rhode Island Almanack
c. Poor Richard's Almanack

William Faulkner and William Falkner, the latter the author of The White Rose of Memphis

I failed my first year examinations at Princeton, ran away to discover the waterfronts of the world, came back to attend drama school at Harvard, and eventually won a Nobel Prize for Literature. Who am I?

The muckraking era beginning in the early 20th century was characterized by its attack on corruption in business and politics. Upton Sinclair's *The Jungle,* about the Chicago meat packing industry, remains the most notable example of this movement.

Who were the authors of the following books and what were the objects of their muckraking?

a. *The Octopus*
b. *The Bitter Cry of the Children*
c. *The Pit*

Two important 20th-century American novelists have been affectionately known as "Red." Who are they?

Eugene O'Neill

Frank Norris wrote both The Octopus *and* The
Pit; *the first focuses on railroad monopolies
(and wheat farmers), the second on the Chicago
grain market. John Spargo wrote* The Bitter
Cry of the Children *about tenement conditions.*

---

*Sinclair Lewis, who got his nickname from the
color of his hair, which he said was "like a new
copper cent," wrote a number of best-selling
novels satirizing the arid materialism and in-
tolerance of American small-town life. His
novel* Babbitt *still lends its title as a synonym
for middle-class American philistinism. Robert
Penn Warren, also a "Red" by virtue of his hair,
has been as prolific and wide-ranging a writer
as any American of this century.*

Which 19th-century American writer was so ashamed of his first two books that he withdrew the first one from circulation and burned the second one before publication?

Which late 19th-century American writer married the madame of a brothel in Florida, was the subject of slanderous rumors about drug addiction and satanism, and died of tuberculosis in Germany at the age of 28?

Students at Harvard within a few years of each other, these two young men set out to travel—partly for their health, but more to cure their wanderlust—in different directions. One became a seaman on a merchant ship bound for California; the other traversed the Great Plains to consort with the Indians and experience the buffalo hunt. On returning, both men published accounts of their journeys which gained immediate popularity and have become recognized travel classics. Who were these two men and what are the titles of their works?

Nathaniel Hawthorne had to pay out of his own pocket for the publication of his first work Fanshawe *(1828), a historical novel, which he immediately took great pains to suppress. Soon after, problems with finding a publisher for a collection of tales he was writing moved him to burn, in chagrin,* Seven Tales of My Native Land.

Stephen Crane—author of The Red Badge of Courage—*was the colorful, and unfortunate, writer.*

Francis Parkman's account of his trip over the eastern part of the Oregon Trail was first serialized in The Knickerbocker Magazine *(1847), and later issued in book form as* The California and Oregon Trail *(1849). The original title,* The Oregon Trail, *was resumed in later editions.*

Richard Henry Dana's account of life at sea and a trip around the Cape Horn, Two Years Before the Mast, *was published anonymously in 1840. It immediately became a great success, and its realism is supposed to have had a great effect on writers of his time, notably Herman Melville.*

∽ Politicking ∽

📖📖————————————————————

"Society is produced by our wants, and government by our wickedness; the former promotes our happiness positively by uniting our affections, the latter negatively by restraining our vices." What 18th-century agitator wrote this and in what book of his does it appear?

📖📖————————————————————

Thomas Paine's *Common Sense* helped forward the cause of the American Revolution; Harriet Beecher Stowe's *Uncle Tom's Cabin* won sympathizers to the side of the Abolitionists before the Civil War; and Upton Sinclair's *The Jungle* was of great social consequence during the Progressive era. What cause did Sinclair's novel help to advance?

Thomas Paine wrote this in his pamphlet entitled Common Sense.

Published in 1906 and depicting life surrounding Chicago's factories and slaughterhouses, Upton Sinclair's The Jungle *aroused the indignation of the public and contributed to the passage of the pure food and drug laws.*

■■————————————————————

This police reporter turned social reformer
fought for the elimination of slum conditions on
New York's Lower East Side during the years at
the turn of the century. One of the first persons
to use the camera as a means of documentation,
he published an illustrated book which raised
public consciousness (as we would say today)
about slum life, and led to far-reaching reform.
Theodore Roosevelt called him "the most useful
citizen of New York" and the title of his work
was so apt it has come to be a cliché. Name this
author and the title of his book.

■■————————————————————

An ardent idealist who founded the Socialist
League, this poet and craftsman battled against
the machine in Victorian England. A member of
the Pre-Raphaelite brotherhood, he also
founded a printing press. Give his name and the
name of his press.

■————————————————————

What do a book-length poem by Tennyson, a
Broadway musical, and the administration of a
recent president have in common?

Jacob Riis wrote How the Other Half Lives.

William Morris founded the Kelmscott Press, a cooperative publishing and printing enterprise on his country estate, in 1891. Its publications are much prized for their beauty of paper, binding and typography.

The theme of Camelot

◧◧◧————————————————————

James Madison believed that this author's essays were "the best that had been written for cherishing in young minds a desire of improvement, a taste for learning, and a lively sense of the duties, the virtues, and the proprieties of life." Satirized by Alexander Pope as "Atticus," this writer held a lifetime parliamentary seat from Malmesbury. Who was he?

◧◧————————————————————————

In 1906 President Theodore Roosevelt applied to the ever-growing group of reformers, social workers and journalists engaged in uncovering corruption in American society the epithet "muckrakers." Can you name the great allegorical work of English literature from which the term was culled, and which Roosevelt cited on the occasion of its coinage?

◧◧————————————————————————

To succeed in one field is rare, but to triumph in both politics and playwriting is truly remarkable. Born in Dublin, this man later bought Garrick's share of Drury Lane and wrote a superb comedy of manners in 1777. He also served with distinction in Parliament. Unfortunately, he utterly failed at handling his own finances and died in penury. Who was he?

It was Joseph Addison who was satirized as "Atticus" by Alexander Pope and who held the safe parliamentary seat of Malmesbury.

The term "muckrakers" comes from The Pilgrim's Progress *by John Bunyan, in which the man with the muck-rake was offered the celestial crown in return for his muck-rake. But he disregarded the offer and continued to rake the filth off the floor.*

Richard Brinsley Sheridan succeeded in both politics and playwriting. His most famous play is The School for Scandal.

～ Battle ～ of the Books

The first novel by this colorful contemporary American novelist chronicles the invasion of Anopoei, a tiny island in the Pacific, during World War II. The author explores the fog of war from two vantage points, that of General Cummings, the commander of the forces making the landing, and of Sergeant Croft, the leader of a platoon sent off on reconnaissance mission. Name the author and the title of his book.

Today the nuclear threat terrifies the world, but an earlier account of the detonation of an atomic bomb shocked America when it first appeared in *The New Yorker* magazine on August 31, 1946. Who wrote this article and what was its title?

Norman Mailer is the author of The Naked and the Dead.

In his article entitled "Hiroshima" in the August 31, 1946, issue of The New Yorker, *John Hersey described the atomic bombing of Hiroshima.*

■

Captain of the frigate H.M.S. *Lydia,* this intrepid naval warrior defeats the *Natividad* not once but twice in a ship-to-ship action, in addition to wooing the spirited sister of the Iron Duke himself. Who created this sea dog and in what book?

■

The year was 1929 and although the boom was about to go bust in America, book sales were mounting. The number-one best seller in fiction that year was an antiwar novel about World War I, copies of which were later burned by the Nazis. What was the name of this best seller and who was its author?

■■

Who wanted and received "a little touch of Harry in the night" and where?

C.S. Forester created Captain Horatio Hornblower, the sea dog whose adventures are first chronicled in Beat to Quarters.

All Quiet on the Western Front, *by Erich Maria Remarque*

The English troops before the battle of Agincourt in Act IV of Shakespeare's Henry V

■■———————————————————

Many notable characters in fiction have held
military rank, for instance Major Major in
Catch-22. What is the rank of each of the following characters and in what novel does each appear?

a. Queeg
b. Cantwell
c. Kutuzov
d. Prewitt

■■■———————————————————

In the years prior to World War I, the military
and naval general staffs of all the great powers
were greatly influenced by two 19th-century
theorists of war. One was an American who
wrote about naval strategy, the other was a
Prussian who said that war was a continuation
of policy by other means. Name these two think-
ers and their most famous books.

a. Lieutenant Commander Queeg, The Caine Mutiny
b. Colonel Cantwell, Across the River and Into the Trees
c. General Kutuzov, War and Peace
d. Private Prewitt, From Here to Eternity

Alfred Thayer Mahan, author of The Influence of Sea Power Upon History, *and Karl von Clausewitz, author of* On War

∼ Roots ∼

The American classic *The Fannie Farmer Cookbook* is associated with what city and cooking school?

Jefferson is the county seat of what fictional rural area made famous by one of America's greatest novelists?

What do all these American books have in common?

Robert Penn Warren's *Night Rider*
Jesse Stuart's *Taps for Private Tussie*
Harriet Arnow's *Hunter's Horn*
Elizabeth Madox Roberts' *The Great Meadow*

The Boston Cooking School in Boston

Yoknapatawpha County was created by William Faulkner as the setting for much of his fiction. Jefferson is patterned after Oxford, Mississippi.

They are all set in Kentucky.

The title of this novel, about a talented writer who loses his family and eventually his life because his books do not sell, harks back to one of the most famous literary locations of 18th-century London. Name the author and the title.

Carl Sandburg called this American city "Hog Butcher for the World." James T. Farrell used it as the setting for his Studs Lonigan trilogy, and William Vaughn Moody described it as:

Gigantic, willful, young,
———————— sitteth at the northwest gates,
With restless violent hands and casual
    tongue
Molding her mighty fates.

What place is he describing?

George Gissing (1857-1903) wrote many novels about the perils of penury. Perhaps his most famous is New Grub Street *(1891), which harked back to the street in London which, during Dr. Johnson's day, was largely inhabited by hack writers of various types.*

Chicago, Illinois

◪◪◪

Poets have always understood the agony of exile.
What native Baltimorean wrote the following
poem which was turned into a Civil War song?

Hark to an exiled son's appeal
Maryland, my Maryland!
Mother State to thee I kneel.

◪◪

In what works, which appeared in the year indi-
cated, do the visions of the following utopias appear?

a. Shangri-La, 1933
b. El Dorado, 1759
c. Bensalem, 1627
d. Erewhon, 1872

◪◪

Prep schools: some would say the best and
others would say the worst days of their lives
were spent there. Name the prep schools that
figure in the following novels:

a. *The Catcher in the Rye,* by J.D. Salinger
b. *A Separate Peace,* by John Knowles
c. *Stalky & Co,* by Rudyard Kipling
d. *Tom Brown's School Days,* by Thomas
   Hughes

At the outbreak of the Civil War, James Ryder Randall, inspired by Baltimore anti-Union sentiment, wrote his famous poem "Maryland, My Maryland."

---

a. *James Hilton's* Lost Horizon
b. *Voltaire's* Candide
c. *Francis Bacon's* The New Atlantis
d. *Samuel Butler's* Erewhon

---

a. *Pencey Prep, Agerstown, Pennsylvaniā*
b. *Devon Academy*
c. *United Services College, Westward Ho, Bideford, North Devon*
d. *Rugby*

∾ Genre Games ∾

◖◗◖◗◖◗————————————————

The Science Fiction Encyclopedia defines an "alternate world" as "an image of Earth as it might be, consequent upon some hypothetical alteration in history." In a novel by Keith Roberts, Roman Catholicism still rules in a technologically backward England because of the assassination of Elizabeth I. Another novel, by Ward Moore, describes a world in which Lee triumphs at Gettysburg and the South wins the Civil War. And in a Hugo award winner, Philip K. Dick has the Allies lose World War II. Name these novels of alternative worlds.

Pavane, *by Keith Roberts*
Come the Jubilee, *by Ward Moore*
The Man in the High Castle, *by Philip K. Dick*

When the lame Sheriff of Selkirkshire penned his first novel, subtitled " 'Tis Sixty Years Since," he created not only what may be the most influential novel of the 19th century, but also a new literary genre as well. What was the name of the novel, the genre, and the author?

This satire on the Gothic romance was sold to a publisher in 1803 for £10. It went unpublished, was bought back by the author's family, and was not actually published until 1818, one year after the author's death. Identify the satire and the satirist.

One of the most important science-fiction novels of the 1950s had a plot that loosely parallels that of *The Count of Monte Cristo* by Alexandre Dumas. What is the name of the novel, and who is its author?

Sir Walter Scott's Waverley *began the rage for the historical novel.*

Northanger Abbey, *by Jane Austen*

Alfred *Bester's* The Stars My Destination, *which won the first Hugo award, was modeled after Dumas's* The Count of Monte Cristo. *Told in a breathless march-time, it is peopled by grotesques and vengeance seekers.*

∾ Grand Finale: ∾
Four-Book Questions

▐▌▐▌▐▌▐▌————————————————

The name of a food completes all these titles.
Can you supply the food and the author?

The Triumph of the ---------
A Few ------from Thistles
-------Face
The ------Tree Table
The Cow's in the -------

The Triumph of the Egg, *by Sherwood Anderson*
A Few Figs from Thistles, *by Edna St. Vincent Millay*
Potato Face, *by Carl Sandburg*
The Apple Tree Table, *by Herman Melville*
The Cow's in the Corn, *by Robert Frost*

◖◗◖◗

Despite intermittent rumors that the novel is dead, most would say that this adaptable form is going strong and that its lease on life may even be infinite. Here are what a few novelists have said about their chosen genre. Can you identify them?

a. "It is with fiction as with religion. It should present another world, but one to which we feel the tie."

b. "It is the first necessity of the novelist's position that he make himself pleasant."

c. "Maybe every novelist wants to write poetry first."

d. The novelist must "Try to be one of the people on whom nothing is lost."

e. "The novel is the one bright book of life."

1. *Herman Melville*
2. *Anthony Trollope*
3. *William Faulkner*
4. *Henry James*
5. *D.H. Lawrence*